Better Homes and Gardens®

T·R·E·A·S·U·R·Y
OF
COUNTRY
CRAFTS AND FOODS

nson
Olson

e in
dorsed by
Each recipe is
iciousness.

BETTER HOMES AND GARDENS® BOOKS

Editor: Gerald M. Knox
Art Director: Ernest Shelton
Managing Editor: David A. Kirchner

Crafts Editor: Nancy Lindemeyer
Crafts Books Editor: Joan Cravens
Associate Crafts Books Editors: Debra Felton, Laura Holtorf,
James A. Williams

Food and Nutrition Editor: Doris Eby
Department Head—Cook Books: Sharyl Heiken
Senior Food Editor: Elizabeth Woolever
Senior Associate Food Editors: Sandra Granseth,
Rosemary C. Hutchinson
Associate Food Editors: Jill Burmeister, Julia Malloy,
Linda Henry, Alethea Sparks, Marcia Stanley, Diane Yanney
Recipe Development Editor: Marion Viall
Test Kitchen Director: Sharon Stilwell
Test Kitchen Home Economists: Jean Brekke, Kay Cargill,
Marilyn Cornelius, Maryellyn Krantz, Marge Steenson

Associate Art Director (Managing): Randall Yontz
Associate Art Directors (Creative): Linda Ford, Neoma Alt West
Copy and Production Editors: Nancy Nowiszewski,
Lamont Olson, Mary Helen Schiltz, David A. Walsh
Assistant Art Directors: Faith Berven, Ha
Graphic Designers: Mike Burns, Alisann Dixo
Lynda Haupert, Deb Miner, Lyne N
D. Greg Thompson

Editor in Chief: Neil Kuehnl
Group Editorial Services Director: Dua

General Manager: Fred Stines
Director of Publishing: Robert B. N
Director of Retail Marketing: Jamie
Director of Direct Marketing: Arthur H

Treasury of Country Crafts and F
Crafts Editor: Ann Levine
Food Editor: Rosemary C. Hutchi
Copy and Production Editor: Lamon
Graphic Designer: Faith Berve